SCIENCE AROUND US

Insects

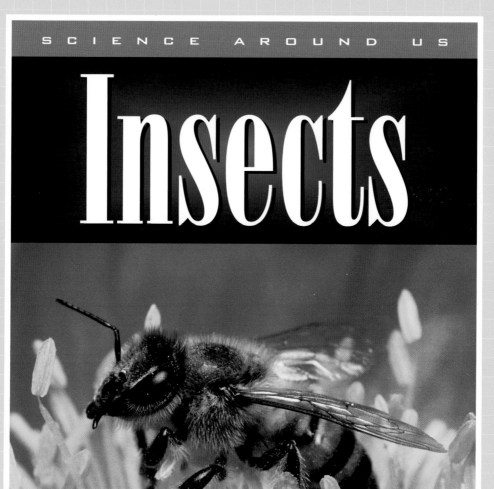

By Peter Murray

THE CHILD'S WORLD®
CHANHASSEN, MINNESOTA

The Child's World

Published in the United States of America by The Child's World®
PO Box 326, Chanhassen, MN 55317-0326
800-599-READ
www.childsworld.com

Content Advisers:
Jim Rising, PhD,
Professor of Zoology,
University of Toronto,
Department of Zoology,
Toronto, Ontario,
Canada, and Trudy
Rising, Educational
Consultant, Toronto,
Ontario, Canada

Photo Credits:
Cover/frontispiece: Anthony Bannister; Gallo Images/Corbis; cover corner: Ralph A.
Clevenger/Corbis.

Interior: Animals Animals/Earth Scenes: 8 (Ruth Cole), 11 (ABPL Image Library), 20
(Raymond Mendez), 23 (Michael Fogden), 25 (Carroll W. Perkins); Corbis: 6 (David
Aubrey), 10 (Clouds Hill Imaging Ltd.), 12 (Michael & Patricia Fogden), 14 (Anthony
Bannister; Gallo Images), 29 (Don Mason); Dembinsky Photo Associates: 7 (Skip
Moody), 13 (Dominique Braud), 16 (Richard Shiell), 18 (Gary Meszaros), 19 (Mark J.
Thomas), 21 (Ed Kanze), 22 (E. R. Degginger), 27 (Jim Battles); Dwight R. Kuhn: 5.

The Child's World®: Mary Berendes, Publishing Director

Editorial Directions, Inc.: E. Russell Primm, Editorial Director; Pam Rosenberg, Line
Editor; Katie Marsico, Assistant Editor; Matt Messbarger, Editorial Assistant; Susan
Hindman, Copy Editor; Susan Ashley, Proofreader; Peter Garnham, Terry Johnson,
Olivia Nellums, Katherine Trickle, and Stephen Carl Wender, Fact Checkers; Tim
Griffin/IndexServ, Indexer; Cian Loughlin O'Day, Photo Researcher; Linda S. Koutris,
Photo Selector

The Design Lab: Kathleen Petelinsek, Design and Page Production

Library of Congress Cataloging-in-Publication Data
Murray, Peter.
  Insects / by Peter Murray.
      p. cm. — (Science around us)
  Includes bibliographical references (p.   ).
  ISBN 1-59296-215-7 (library bound : alk. paper) 1. Insects—Juvenile literature.
I. Title. II. Science around us (Child's World (Firm))
  QL467.2.M886 2004
  595.7—dc22   2004000586

TABLE OF CONTENTS

CHAPTER ONE

WHAT IS AN INSECT?

Insects first appeared on Earth about 400 million years ago. Since then, they have evolved into a bewildering assortment of colors, shapes, and sizes. Some, like the goliath beetle, are as big as your hand. Others are so tiny that you need a magnifying glass to see them. But all insects are closely related, and all have certain things in common.

Millions of years ago, some insects were trapped in sticky sap. The sap hardened, which permanently locked in the insects. These preserved specimens show us what insects looked like back in the days of the dinosaurs.

BODY ARMOR

Insects belong to a group of armored animals called arthropods. Spiders, scorpions, and lobsters also belong to this group. Insects, like other arthropods, have no backbone or internal skeleton.

Adult arthropods are protected by an exoskeleton, or shell, made

The short-horned grasshopper has short antennae, or horns.

of **chitin.** The exoskeleton covers the insect's entire body, from its

feet to the tips of its **antennae.** Even its eyes are coated with a

thin layer of clear chitin.

SIX LEGS

The easiest way to tell if an animal is an insect is to count its legs.

Centipedes and millipedes are not insects. They are more closely related to lobsters and crabs. Centipedes and millipedes have been around for longer than the insects. They were among the first animals to move from the oceans and ponds onto dry land.

If an animal has eight legs, it is probably a spider. If it has many legs, it might be a millipede. Spiders and millipedes are not insects. But if an animal has exactly six legs, it is probably an insect.

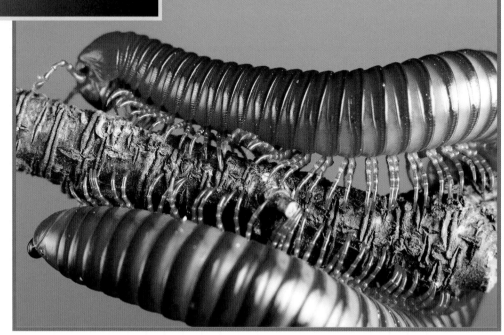

Even though they have many legs, millipedes are slow-moving creatures.

FOUR WINGS

Insects were the first animals that could fly. Most insects have four wings, although some **species** have lost one or both pairs of wings over time.

THREE SEGMENTS

The body of an adult insect is divided into three segments. The first segment is the head. The head carries an insect's eyes, brain, mouth, and antennae.

Most insects, such as this dragonfly, have four wings. Dragonflies can flap each pair of wings independently—one pair can be moving up while the other is moving down.

Each insect eye is made up of hundreds of tiny lenses. To us, looking through an insect eye would be like looking through a kaleidoscope. The insect brain is able to sort out all the light and color.

*If you look closely at the long antennae of this red milkweed beetle,
you can see they are made up of many segments.*

Insect mouths vary according to an insect's diet and way of feeding. The preying mantis has powerful jaws designed for tearing apart other insects. Houseflies have spongy "lips" designed for sucking up liquids. Butterflies have long, coiled tongues for reaching deep into flowers. Mosquitoes have a hollow, needlelike mouth—and you know what they do with that!

Antennae are one of an insect's most important parts. Antennae can detect odors, sound, taste, air movement, temperature, and humidity.

The middle segment of an insect's body is called the thorax. The thorax is the insect's engine. Its strong muscles power the insect's wings and legs which are attached to it.

The abdomen is the third and largest segment. This is where you will find the insect's heart, digestive system, and reproductive

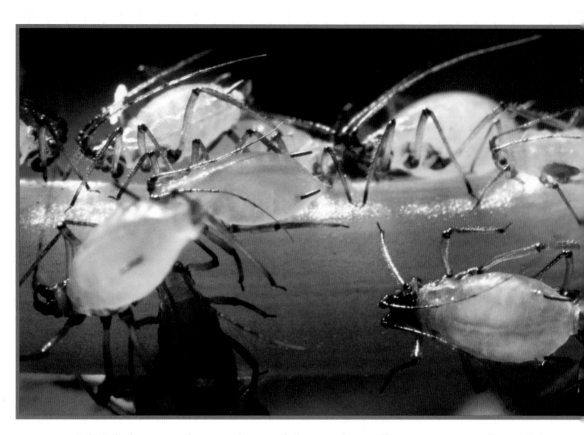

Aphids feed on young leaves and stems of plants and give off a sugary waste product called honeydew. Bees, wasps, and ants collect honeydew for food.

organs. The abdomen also contains air sacs and has several small holes on the sides for breathing.

All three body parts of the insect work together—the head for seeing and eating, the thorax for walking and flying, and the abdomen for digestion, breathing, and reproducing. From the goliath beetle to the tiny aphid, all insects are built on this same basic plan.

CHAPTER TWO

METAMORPHOSIS

A few hundred years ago, people thought that the flies and **maggots** feeding on a dead animal had come from inside

the dead body. But people just did not understand how insects

reproduce.

These wormlike creatures are housefly larvae, or maggots.

A butterfly lays its tiny, yellow eggs on a leaf.

In 1668, an Italian scientist named Francesco Redi put pieces of rotting meat in three jars. He covered one jar with glass and one with fine netting. He left the third jar open. Redi watched as flies landed in the open jar and laid tiny eggs on the meat. Soon, the meat in the open jar was covered with maggots. No maggots appeared on the other two pieces of meat.

Redi proved that flies and other insects do not appear as if by magic from rotting meat. Like birds, frogs, and fish, insects reproduce by laying eggs.

Insects grow from egg to adult in a process called metamor-

phosis. One spectacular example of metamorphosis is the monarch

butterfly.

Monarch butterflies migrate hundreds of miles to spend the winter in warm climates. Sometimes large groups of monarch butterflies can be seen resting in trees along their migration route.

A monarch butterfly caterpillar feeds on milkweed. This is why monarch butterflies are sometimes called milkweed butterflies.

The adult monarch butterfly lays an egg on the underside of a milkweed leaf. In a few days, the egg hatches into a tiny **larva** no larger than a comma. The larva begins eating immediately. It grows quickly. Within a couple of weeks, it has grown into a caterpillar about the size of your little finger.

Once the caterpillar reaches full size, it changes again, encasing itself in a protective shell. This stage is called the chrysalis, or pupa.

Inside its shell, the caterpillar begins to change. In about two weeks, the thin shell splits open and an adult butterfly comes out, ready to make and lay eggs of its own.

Flies, bees, ants, beetles, and moths go through a similar four-step cycle: from egg to larvae to pupa to adult.

Dragonflies, grasshoppers, and many other insects take a different path called incomplete metamorphosis—they do not go through larval and pupal stages.

Dragonflies hatch as tiny six-legged, wingless, water-breathing

Dragonfly nymphs eat mosquito larvae and other insects, as well as larger animals such as tadpoles.

nymphs. The nymphs live under water for the first two to three years. As the nymphs get bigger, they shed their exoskeleton several times. Finally, the nymph sheds its skin one last time and becomes a full-sized, winged adult dragonfly.

CHAPTER THREE

THE SOCIAL INSECTS

Most insects live solitary lives, coming together only to mate.

But ants, termites, bees, and wasps live in nests in which

each individual insect works for the survival of the **colony.**

A group of Apache wasps builds a nest.

BEES AND WASPS

These related insects are known for building large nests, or hives.

One honeybee hive might contain a queen bee, a few hundred male

bees, or drones, and about 60,000 female "worker bees." The queen

bee lays all the eggs, while the worker bees gather food, build the

wax honeycomb, and feed the young larvae.

Social wasps build their nests from paper they make by chewing

up bits of wood. Some wasps make large, football-shaped nests.

Others build their nests inside trees or

walls. The common yellow jacket often

nests underground.

Not all bees and wasps live in

colonies. Many species, such as tarantula

hawks and carpenter bees, live alone.

What's the difference between bees and wasps? Bees have lots of fuzzy hair on their bodies; wasps have smooth abdomens. Bees feed their larvae honey and nectar; wasps often feed their larvae meat. Bees can sting only once; wasps can sting repeatedly.

A wasp kills a cicada. Wasps are helpful to farmers because they kill insects that can damage crops.

Many people fear bees and wasps. No one likes to get stung.

But bees and wasps are some of our most useful insects. Bees provide

us with honey and help **pollinate** crops. Wasps aid farmers by

killing caterpillars, flies, and other damaging insects.

ANTS

Ants are closely related to bees and wasps. With more than 9,000 species of ants worldwide, they have adapted to life in almost every environment.

Most ants live in colonies. Each colony has an egg-laying queen, a small number of male ants, and many thousands of female workers. The

Leaf-cutter ants bring pieces of leaves into their nests. They don't eat the leaves—they use them as a garden for growing an edible fungus.

Millions of leaf-cutter ants can live in a single colony.

Worker ants care for the colony's young larvae. In an ant colony, each ant has a specific job.

workers are often designed to do different jobs within the same

nest—some care for the young larvae, some bring food into the nest,

and others have powerful jaws for defending the nest.

Ants eat a wide variety of foods, from flower nectar to leaves to

other insects.

TERMITES

Termites are common in warmer climates, but unless you break into one of their nests, you might never see one. Termites avoid sunlight. Most spend their entire lives underground or in nests made of dirt and saliva.

Like ants and bees, termite colonies contain different types of termites—workers, soldiers, males, and a single queen. Worker termites are small, usually less than $^1/_2$ centimeter ($^1/_4$ inch) long. Termite queens can be quite large—up to 10 centimeters (4 inches) long. A queen can lay as many as 30,000 eggs per day.

Termite mounds sometimes look like tall towers. The older the mound, the larger it is in size.

CHAPTER FOUR

BEETLES, BUGS, AND FLIES

BEETLES

Adult beetles are the armored cars of the insect world. The beetle's front wings form a hard shell that covers its abdomen. The rear wings are folded underneath.

About one-third of all insect species are beetles. Beetles come in a wide variety of shapes, sizes, and colors. The tanklike goliath beetle can grow to be nearly 15 centimeters (6 inches) long. The nearly invisible feather-winged beetle can be smaller than the period at the end of this sentence.

The atlas beetle, like all beetles, has front wings that form a hard shell to protect its abdomen.

Like all weevils, this brush-snouted weevil from Costa Rica has a long snout.

Each beetle species has adapted to different foods and different environments. Tiger beetles chase and devour other insects—they are built for speed. The giraffe beetle's head is designed to fit deep into cracks where it finds its food.

BUGS

Most of us call just about any insect a bug. But true bugs are members of a special group of insects. These bugs have a tubelike mouth that can stab and suck the juices from plants or animals. Examples of true bugs include cicadas, bedbugs, and giant water bugs.

FLIES

Flies are insects with only one pair of wings. All other flying insects have four wings. Hundreds of millions of years ago, flies dropped their "extra" pair of wings.

Today, there are more than 120,000 species of flies. Many fly species are serious pests. Horseflies, blackflies, midges, gnats, mosquitoes, and other biting flies can ruin a picnic in no time. Some, like the medfly, damage crops. Tsetse flies, botflies, and mosquitoes carry diseases that harm tens of millions of people every year. Even the common housefly can carry diseases such as typhoid and cholera.

Not all flies are harmful. Many species are important for pollinating plants. Blowflies lay their eggs on dead animals. The blowfly larvae help break down the dead flesh and return it to the earth. Robber flies and other **predator** flies attack and eat other insects, helping keep the number of crop pests under control. Many kinds of birds rely on flies for food.

The mosquito is a type of fly. One of the world's most dangerous insects, some species of mosquitoes spread malaria, yellow fever, and other deadly diseases.

Only female mosquitos bite humans. They need the protein in blood for their eggs.

CHAPTER FIVE

BUTTERFLIES AND MOTHS

Butterflies and moths are closely related. They have large, often colorful wings. All moths and butterflies undergo a complete metamorphosis.

Butterflies and moths do most of their eating while they are in the caterpillar stage. Some caterpillars damage crops and forests. A single tomato hornworm, which is the larva of the sphinx moth, can destroy an entire tomato plant. The gypsy moth caterpillar is a serious forest pest, destroying thousands of acres of woodland every year.

Adult butterflies and moths do not eat

What's the difference between butterflies and moths? Butterflies fly by day; moths usually fly at night. Butterflies are usually colorful; many moths are dull in color. Butterfly antennae have tiny knobs at the end; moth antennae come in a variety of shapes and don't have knobs at the end. Butterflies rest with their wings up; moths rest with their wings flat.

A postman butterfly sips nectar. Adult butterflies only drink nectar or juice from rotting fruit.

solid food. They use their coiled, hollow "tongue" to sip flower nectar or juice from rotting fruit.

◆ ◆ ◆

A few species we have not mentioned are the cockroaches, lice, and walking sticks. But there are far too many types of insects to cover in any one book. More than 1 million insects have been named, but **entomologists** believe that millions more remain to be discovered. Maybe you or a friend will discover some when you grow up!

GLOSSARY

antennae (an-TEH-nae) Antennae are the feelers on the head of an insect.

chitin (KYE-ten) Chitin is the hard, clear substance that forms a shell, or exoskeleton, around an insect's body.

colony (KOL-uh-nee) A colony is a large group of insects that live together and depend on each other for survival.

entomologists (en-tuh-MOL-oh-jists) Entomologists are scientists who study insects.

larva (LAR-vuh) A larva is an insect at the stage of development between egg and pupa when it looks similar to a worm. A caterpillar is the larva of a moth or a butterfly.

maggots (MAG-uhts) Maggots are the larvae, or young, of some kinds of insects.

pollinate (POL-uh-nate) To pollinate means to carry pollen from the male part of a flower to the female part of a flower, so that the plant can produce seeds.

predator (PRED-uh-tur) A predator is an animal that hunts other animals for food.

species (SPEE-sheez) A species is a certain type of living thing. Insects of the same species can mate and produce young. Insects of different species cannot produce young together.

▶ Fleas lost their wings many millions of years ago. Instead of flying, the flea uses its powerful legs to jump from place to place.

▶ Honeybees build small cells with wax walls for storing honey and pollen. The cells are also used for growing the young larvae.

▶ The female tarantula hawk stings a tarantula, then lays a single egg on its paralyzed body. When the egg hatches, the wasp larva feeds on the stunned spider.

▶ The giant water bug can grow to 10 centimeters (4 inches) long. It feeds on insects, fish, worms, and small amphibians.

▶ The common housefly feeds by "spitting" on its food. The saliva dissolves the food. The fly then sucks it up with its spongelike mouth.

▶ The Malaysian walking stick is the longest insect known. It measures up to 56 centimeters (22 inches) long.

▶ African termite nests can be up to 6 meters (20 feet) tall and contain more than 1 million termites..

Beekeepers use human-made hives to raise bees for their honey.

▶ The world's largest butterfly, the Queen Alexandra's Birdwing, has a wingspan of up to 30 centimeters (12 inches). It lives in the rain forests of Papua New Guinea.

THE ANIMAL KINGDOM

VERTEBRATES

fish

amphibians

reptiles

birds

mammals

INVERTEBRATES

sponges

worms

insects

spiders & scorpions

mollusks & crustaceans

sea stars

sea jellies

HOW TO LEARN MORE ABOUT INSECTS

At the Library
Greenaway, Theresa. *Big Book of Bugs.* New York: DK Publishing, 2000.

Jackson, Donna M. *Bug Scientist.* New York: Houghton Mifflin, 2002.

Kneidel, Sally. *More Pet Bugs: A Kid's Guide to Catching and Keeping Insects and Other Small Creatures.* New York: John Wiley & Sons, 1999.

Mound, Lawrence, Colin Keates, and Frank Greenaway (photographers). *Eyewitness: Insect.* New York: DK Publishing, 2000.

On the Web
VISIT OUR HOME PAGE FOR LOTS OF LINKS ABOUT INSECTS:
http://www.childsworld.com/links.html
Note to Parents, Teachers, and Librarians: We routinely check our Web links to make sure they're safe, active sites—so encourage your readers to check them out!

Places to Visit or Contact
PEGGY NOTEBAERT NATURE MUSEUM
To see many different kinds of butterflies in the Judy Istock Butterfly Haven
2430 North Cannon Drive
Chicago, IL 60614
773/755-5100

SMITHSONIAN NATIONAL MUSEUM OF NATURAL HISTORY
To visit the O. Orkin Insect Zoo exhibit and learn more about insects
10th Street and Constitution Avenue NW
Washington, DC 20560
202/357-2700

INDEX

About the Author

Peter Murray has written more than 80 children's books on science, nature, history, and other topics. An animal lover, Pete lives in Golden Valley, Minnesota, in a house with one woman, two poodles, several dozen spiders, thousands of microscopic dust mites, and an occasional mouse.